CW00666016

Novels for Students, Volume 42

Project Editor: Sara Constantakis **Rights Acquisition and Management**: Christine Myaskovsky **Composition**: Evi Abou-El-Seoud **Manufacturing**: Rhonda Dover

Imaging: John Watkins

Product Design: Pamela A. E. Galbreath, Jennifer Wahi **Digital Content Production**: Allie Semperger **Product Manager**: Meggin Condino © 2013 Gale, Cengage Learning

For product information and technology assistance, contact us at **Gale Customer Support, 1-800-877-4253.**

For permission to use material from this text or product, submit all requests online at www.cengage.com/permissions.

Further permissions questions can be emailed to **permissionrequest@cengage.com**   While every effort has been made to ensure the reliability of the information presented in this publication, Gale, a part of Cengage Learning, does not guarantee the accuracy of the data contained herein. Gale accepts no payment for listing; and inclusion in the publication of any organization, agency, institution, publication, service, or individual does not imply endorsement of the editors or publisher. Errors brought to the attention of the publisher and verified to the satisfaction of the publisher will be corrected in future editions.

Gale
27500 Drake Rd.
Farmington Hills, MI, 48331-3535

ISBN-13: 978-1-4144-9485-2
ISBN-10: 1-4144-9485-8
ISSN 1094-3552

This title is also available as an e-book.

ISBN-13: 978-1-4144-9271-1
ISBN-10: 1-4144-9271-5
Contact your Gale, a part of Cengage Learning sales
representative for ordering information.

Printed in Mexico
1 2 3 4 5 6 7 17 16 15 14 13

The Arrival

Shaun Tan 2006

Introduction

Shaun Tan's 2006 *The Arrival* may be a new experience for many readers. It tells its story of immigrants setting out to build new lives in a new country entirely without words, using only pictures. The serial style of illustration, familiar from comic strips, is pushed to new levels of sophistication in the relatively new format of the graphic novel. Each panel is meticulously drawn in a photo-realistic style that purposefully imitates photos pasted in an album (a form that itself will soon be a thing of the past), but incorporates unreal and allegorical elements of monsters and impossible landscapes out of the world of dreams. Tan mixes styles from comic books and surrealism and from history and science fiction to create a world that is as fantastic as it is familiar. *The Arrival* contains an unreadable language, unbelievable creatures, and a warm embrace of home and family. The reader's own imagination must be used to create meaning from the book's images.

Note that Tan wrote a summary of *The Arrival* for the Scholastic website (http://www.scool.scholastic.com.au/schoolzone/too that provides valuable information about his view of the novel's plot and characters.

Author Biography

Tan was born in Perth, Australia, on the first day of 1974. His parents were ethnic Chinese immigrants to Australia from Malaysia, where his ancestors had long ago immigrated from China. Tan's father moved to Australia in 1970, after tight racial restrictions on immigration had been lifted, and found work as an architect. Tan's personal background undoubtedly accounts in part for the interest displayed in his works on immigration as well as Australian history.

Tan began publishing illustrations in science-fiction fanzines and other semiprofessional venues in high school and majored in fine art at the University of Western Australia in Melbourne. He graduated in 1995 and has lived in Melbourne since then. He immediately found success as an illustrator of children's books and has won innumerable Australian and international awards for children's illustration. He quickly became his own writer as well, once he realized that the writer received half of the royalties for producing a few hundred words. Tan achieved his mature style in *The Rabbits* in 1998, mixing elements of classical painting with popular modern themes like steam punk. Although Tan did not write it, *The Rabbits* is an allegory of the colonization of Australia, a mixture of history and the fantastic that would come to dominate his work. He achieved international recognition with *The Lost Thing*. Here he develops themes that would contribute the fantastic elements of *The Arrival*, including a prototype of the father's familiar animal. The Arrival (2006) became his best-received work, being nominated for a Hugo Award at the 2007 World Science Fiction Convention. In 2010 Tan won the Hugo for best artist, in recognition of his entire body of work.

Although Tan has continued to publish illustrated books, most recently *Tales from Outer Suburbia* in 2008 (an anthology of stories set in a familiar suburban world with out-of-place fantastic elements intruding), his interest in narrative and serial illustration has increasingly led him to film work. He worked as a concept artist on the design of the films *Horton Hears a Who* (2008) and *Wall-E* (2008). The work of film directors such as Stanley Kubrick and Terry Gilliam has always been a major influence on Tan's work. In 2009–2010 he directed an animated version of *The Lost Thing*, which won the Oscar for Best Animated Short in 2011. Tan is currently doing preliminary work on a film version of *The Arrival*, but no definite project has yet been announced.

Plot Summary

Because *The Arrival* is a graphic novel, it presents many difficulties that are not encountered in reading an ordinary text. Each page is divided into panels, ranging from one to thirty-six on a page (although some panels take up two pages). Anything from a single panel to several pages may be a grouping equivalent to a chapter or section in an ordinary book. Since the author does not denote any grouping smaller than the six chapters with headings, the reader may be referred to specific section by page number or even references to single panels. Note, however, that page numbers are not marked in the text. For this purpose, the first illustrated page is considered page one.

In general, the text is presented as if it consisted of scans or photographs of an old photo album, including images of the crumpled, torn, or worn pages of the original; even the cover displays an image of a cracked and broken leather spine.

Media Adaptations

- In July 2006, the Spare Parts Puppet Theater staged a production based on *The Arrival* in Freemantle, Australia.

- In 2008, Nick Stathopoulos painted a portrait of Tan in which he holds the father's familiar animal from *The Arrival*.

- In 2009, the Red Leap Theatre in New Zealand staged a production of *The Arrival*.

- In 2010–2011, Ben Walsh and the Orkestra of the Underground Sydney Opera House staged a musical version of *The Arrival* in Sydney and Melbourne.

I (pp. 1–10)

Page 1 shows scenes from a rather poor household, with unpainted wooden walls and cracked china in use. Documents related to an overseas voyage together with a partially packed suitcase suggest a trip. There is a photograph of a young couple and their daughter, as well as drawing of the family by the girl. On pages 2–3, the father packs away the photo of the family in his suitcase. It is clear that he is going away on a journey without his family. On page 4, his wife and daughter nevertheless dress to accompany him part of the way. Pages 5–7 show the rundown neighborhood of row houses where the family lives. Of this sequence, Tan himself says, the city "has strange, enormous serpents moving through the air (for me this is an open metaphor for some kind of oppression or decay)." The father then tearfully leaves his family on a train, giving his daughter an origami bird, and the mother and daughter return home.

II (pp. 11–45)

On page 11, the father is on a steamship, staring wistfully at a portrait of the family he left behind. Pages 12–16 are devoted to the clouds above the ship. Tan exploits the possibilities of pareidolia, the tendency of the human mind to impose patterns on random phenomena such as clouds, with the densest series of panels in the book, each showing a different cloud shape that is evocative and suggestive without yielding any definite meaning.

On pages 17–28, Tan turns toward reproducing famous, and not so famous, images of Ellis Island, the entry point in New York Harbor for many European immigrants to the United States a hundred years ago, but with fantastic elements projected into them. Sitting on the deck of the ship, the father writes in his journal, then tears out a sheet and makes an origami bird. Suddenly a whole flock of apparently origami creatures is flying low over the ship's deck. They have characteristics of fish, birds, and lizards all mixed together. In a single panel splashed over pages 20 and 21, the ship enters what might be New York Harbor: the Empire State Building is recognizable in the background. But the sky is littered with numerous balloons and flying vessels that more closely resemble boats than aircraft, while the surface of the water is pierced by what might be the spires of numerous submerged churches. There is no Statue of Liberty, but rather a monumental statue showing two men in oriental dress shaking hands. One, with a bird perched on his shoulder, appears to be a native welcoming the other, an immigrant (marked by his suitcase) holding a kangaroo-like creature. The remainder of the section is taken up with the more or less realistic process of the medical and other exams that immigrants were put through. Tan also introduced the pseudo-alphabet and language he devised for the book; the father clearly cannot read or speak the associated language. But he is finally passed through and allowed to enter the country.

The father is sent aloft in a balloon to drift over the city (pp. 28–31). The city has realistic elements of a densely built-up urban area, but also has design elements derived from the artistic movements of cubism and futurism. It is heavily industrial, dominated by giant smokestacks. Areas that might seem to be highways or railways, if one follows their path, soon are merely taken up with more buildings. Other buildings seem to float in the air. There is a gigantic anthropomorphic bird with wings and arms holding an egg at which it gazes nervously, but is this a monumental statue or an actual creature? Finally, the balloon lands, dropping the father off in a random part of the city. Pages 34–35 show the snapshots representing the father's impressions of the city, mostly various sorts of street vendors. Almost everyone has a strange familiar animal (some like cats or iguanas or a kind of land-living nautilus). One woman seems to be selling produce in the form of gigantic eggs larger than footballs and a box of tentacles as if they were cuts of beef.

The father cannot read street signs or maps in the foreign language of the city, or converse with its inhabitants. However, he approaches a man in foreign dress (with a mammalian insectivore familiar) and draws in his notebook a picture of a bedroom, in this way asking where he might rent a room. The landlady (who keeps something like a frog with wings and eye-stalks in a sugar jar on the check-out desk) gives him a room. The father examines strange machinery in the room that he doesn't understand, and on pages 40–42 finds an urn housing the animal that will become his companion. At first he chases it like vermin, but then comes to accept it. He sadly remembers his family with the creature looking on. The chapter ends (pp. 44–45), with another fantastic cityscape.

III (pp. 46–77)

The father awakens from a dream of cloudscapes that gradually become his animal sitting on his chest like a cat. He sets out to find work. Waiting at a stop for one of the city's aerial buses, his familiar befriends an owl-like creature, who in turn belongs to a woman who shows the father how to purchase a bus ticket from a vending machine. As they ride together, he shows her his immigration papers, and then she shows him hers. Then (pp. 52–55) her life story is shown. How she explains this to the father since they don't seem to speak the same language is unclear, but the story is told in a series of panels that more closely resemble photographs, with a white border like old prints and showing much wear and damage, while the background pages are darker in color (as if the reader were now looking at pages from her scrap book). In the first panel, she (as a child) attempts to read a book, but this is taken and locked away from her and she is put to work as an industrial slave, tending a furnace. But she managed to steal the book and escape, and made her way to the new city.

On pages 57–60, the father attempts to buy groceries. He again communicates by drawing the items he wants in his notebook (bread, fish, cheese, et cetera), but the grocer can only sell him the local foods, which all seem to be bizarre examples of shellfish. Since the father clearly has no idea how to prepare this food, the grocer's son suggests inviting him home for dinner. On the journey there by boat, the father's animal and the boy's reptilian fox become friends. The father explains his own history, showing his house in his own country with the mysterious tentacles threatening. The grocer then tells his story. The following panels (pp. 64–72) are distinguished from the main story by being printed with a black background. Pages 64–65 show people fleeing through a plaza lined with Renaissance and baroque churches. The more distant part of the city is on fire. Huge cyclopean figures, hundreds of feet tall and dressed in some kind of high-tech jump suits, are wielding vacuum cleaners which suck up the people as well as the stones of the building. The grocer and his wife are among those fleeing, and they escape by going down a manhole. They come back up when the cyclopes have passed, but their city is completely transformed into a mass of threatening geometric shapes like something from a 1920s German expressionist film. They are finally able to escape the city with the help of a man with a lantern, who demands to be paid with the last thing they possess, a piece of the wife's jewelry. They eventually succeed in taking a rowboat on the ocean to escape their homeland.

Returning to the main narrative thread of the novel, the father has dinner with the grocer and his family (pp. 73–77), who live in an area of the city where the architecture is dominated by giant owl sculptures. The dinner is notable for its warmth and hospitality. The father makes an origami fox for the grocer's son. At the end of the dinner, the grocer and his wife offer the father a pot filled with dark liquid.

IV (pp. 78–101)

The next morning, when the father awakens, the first thing he sees is the pot, now empty and sitting on his bedside table back in his room. As he sets out to find work, the father moves through crowds where many people are, like himself, accompanied by their familiar creatures. He sees many street vendors and workers. He asks for work at many establishments (p. 81), but is always turned down. Finally (p. 82), his familiar approaches a sign hanger who is willing to pay him to take over his work for the afternoon. But, unable to read the signs printed in the city's language, he hangs them upside down. He takes another job (pp. 84–89), offered him by a woman who runs a street stall, to work as a deliveryman until he is frightened off one assignment by a giant dragon. At last (pp. 86–87), he finds work in a factory that produces small bottles. He works at a conveyor belt and picks out and throws away any bottles that are imperfect. He works on a gigantic shop floor with hundreds of others doing the same task, with dynamos that are several stories tall spinning in the background. An elderly coworker across the conveyor belt from the father shares something like coffee with him, and, seeing an imperfect bottle, is reminded of the tragedy of his life story (whether this is communicated to the father is not clear). The sequence too is shown on darker pages with more realistic images of photographs.

When the elderly coworker was a young man (pp. 89–95), with a wife or sweetheart, he went off to war with a sense of jubilation, his unit parading through the streets under a rain of flower petals. The conflict he joins is modeled on the First World War, with its terrible assaults across no-man's-land between systems of trenches in the face of artillery and machine-gun fire. The final scene of war shows a blasted field of shell craters littered with human bones. His leg amputated because of wounds suffered in the war, the man returns on crutches to his hometown, only to see it has been reduced to ruins by enemy artillery.

Back in the main narrative, after work, the elderly coworker invites the father and his animal companion, who joins him outside the factory, to go with him (pp. 96–101). As they walk into the countryside just outside the city, the old man takes a small lizard-like creature from his pocket and tosses it into the air where it spreads wings and flies away. The countryside looks more like a park than woods, with what may be a farmer's field, although the crop is not identifiable. It is thick with flying lizard creatures. The sky contains many suns, in some of which can be seen machinery or a gestating human embryo. They join a group of the old man's friends, all of whom are from different countries if not different continents, and all of whom have animal companions, in a sort of bowling game.

V (pp. 102–115)

On pages 103–104, one of the flying lizard creatures picks up a fallen twig from a field and carries it to the father's apartment, where it deposits the twig in the empty jar from the grocer, now sitting on the window sill, which already holds many such bits of detritus. The father (pp. 104–105) writes a letter to his wife, folding the letter into an origami dove and enclosing money. He mails it, and the mail box becomes a balloon and carries the letter to the addressee.

The mailbox was in the middle of a field of giant plants that were a single leaf growing out of the ground to a height of about twelve feet. Now (pp. 106–107) the narrative shows the life cycle of one these plants as it flowers, germinates (producing two cycles of seeds, the first carried away by the wind like a dandelion's, and the second eaten by the lizard-birds), and then dying and rotting away in a deep bank of snow. Then the whole city is shown under a blanket of snow (pp. 108–109).

On pages 110–111, the flying lizard returns to the jar and feeds its three chicks, which live in the jar as a nest while the father gazes longingly at the picture of his family. His animal companion hears the mail arrive and goes to get a letter for the father, which makes him smile and cry with joy when he reads it. It announces that his wife and child are going to join him. They are flying on a balloon and the father races to reach their landing site (pp. 111–115). They are filled with trepidation but smile with joy when they see the father, running to meet him. The embrace of reunion is shown in a giant field spread across two whole pages and from a very distant vantage point so that the figures are tiny and indistinct to the reader.

VI (pp. 116–122)

The final chapter begins (p. 117) with a series of pictures strongly reminiscent of the first page, but clearly set in the family's new apartment in the new city. Page 3, with its sorrowful image of the father's suitcase resting on the dinner table, is reflected in a joyous picture (p. 118) of the family taking breakfast together, along with the animal companion. The scene also visually echoes the happy meal the father had in the home of the grocer (p. 76). In the final sequence of *The Arrival* (pp. 119–122), the child is sent on an errand to buy food from a vending machine, accompanied by the animal companion. She encounters a newly arrived immigrant woman and starts helping her find her way around the city.

Characters

Child

The child of the immigrant family is clearly marked as a girl throughout *The Arrival*. She has softer facial features, longer hair like the other female characters, and wears dresses, although she appears to be about eight or nine years old so no secondary sexual characteristics are present. Nevertheless, Tan, in his summary of the book for Scholastic, uses the neutral word "child," and even uses the masculine pronoun.

She stays with her mother when the father goes to the new country, and only joins him when the family is reunited at the end. But she is the link to the end of the story where she in her turn helps a new immigrant.

Cyclopes

These figures are shown as giants towering over tall buildings as they destroy the grocer's country of origin. They wear clothing that might best be described as costumes from 1950s and 1960s science-fiction films for technicians in nuclear plants. This is an example of retro-futurism, the reuse of a past era's conception of the future in a time when that future has already become the past.

As the cyclopes trample and burn the city, they

suck up people into giant vacuum cleaners strapped to their backs. On the Scholastic website, Tan explains that the cyclopes are "a metaphor for Nazism or Communism." This allows the reader a glimpse into the larger allegorical structure of the novel, or least a view into Tan's imaginative process. The sucking of people into vacuum cleaners represents the horrible death toll cause by Fascist and Communist régimes in the twentieth century through war and acts of genocide. Their destroying of buildings and cities stand for the challenge to civilization posed by those ideologies, not only in the direct destruction they caused through war, but through the intellectual degradation of culture and learning they caused. Tan shows them destroying a group of historic churches, perhaps as a symbol of the destruction of traditional civilization (an alternative, such as art museums, would not have been as recognizable).

Delivery Business Owner

The second job that the father gets is delivering packages around the city for a woman who works out of a stall in a marketplace. While almost all societies in the early twentieth century discouraged women's economic and social independence, the situation of novelty and poverty faced by many immigrant communities cultivated an entrepreneurial spirit in many immigrant women, who often had to support their children alone. This is reflected in this character.

Elderly Coworker

Once the father begins his assembly-line job, he is befriended by an elderly man who works on the conveyor belt across from him. He tells the father the story of the events that led to his own immigration, namely the loss of his family and the destruction of his village in a war (which also cost him his leg) whose graphic presentation is based on photos of the Western Front in World War I. However, on the Scholastic website, Tan describes this conflict as a civil war, highlighting again the mixture of fantastic and real history in the novel.

Ex-Slave

On his first day looking for work, the father is helped by a young woman in navigating the transportation system of the new city. She tells him her story (or at least the reader sees her story; since she and the father don't speak a common language, it is unclear how much of this he could have absorbed). She was, as Tan confirms on the Scholastic website, an industrial slave who managed to escape to the new country. Significantly, her story begins with her master seizing from her and locking away a book, and when she escapes she takes the risk of finding and taking the same book. This is perhaps a metaphor for the role of education in the economic advancement of immigrants.

Father

Despite the fact that the father and his actions are the main focus of the story, his character is not particularly well developed. This is because he acts as a lens through which the reader may experience the world of the new city and all of its novelties for himself. Similarly, the father is an everyman in terms of his appearance. While the other immigrants to the city tend to wear a distinctive, though fictitious, national dress, the father wears a Western suit and fedora that would fit in almost anywhere on Earth during the twentieth century. The father thinks of himself in terms of his relationship to his family and how he can help them. They are never far from his mind, a fact indicated by the frequent presence of the family photo and by his reverie (p. 42), in which he opens his suitcase to take the picture out and hang it in his new apartment, but seems to see his wife and child as if they were present, carrying out their lives in miniature before him. The father is also keen to fit into the new world of his adopted city, both economically, by finding a job that will support his family (tying these two themes together), and socially, by making friendships. Both of these aspects of his new life are necessary for his survival and prosperity. The two worlds of work and social connections also allow him to experience, on behalf of the reader, a wide range of the new city's wonders. Subservient to these goals, the father is a dedicated worker (though he often fails at jobs because of circumstances outside of his control) and is avid to seek out new friends and contacts. His range of friendships not only advances his own goals, but allows the reader to experience more characters and their stories.

Michael D. Boatright, in his 2010 article in the *Journal of Adolescent and Adult Literacy*, describes the immigrant father as a white, Nordic European whose story is used to silence narratives of non-Nordic immigrants to the United States. In fact, however, the father is clearly oriental in appearance, and is, moreover, clearly a self-portrait of Tan. His appearance fits within the broad spectrum of ethnic types that Tan portrays in the harmonious society of the new city.

Father's Animal Companion

Tan has described this creature as a tadpole, while Gene Luen Yang, in his *New York Times* review of *The Arrival*, has likened it to the video game character Packman. The design of the creature was created by a process that may be termed automatic drawing, in which Tan sketched in a very loose manner with no definite intention and finally found its design emerging. The creature's body is, in fact, a shark's head: the pointed snout, binocular eyes, and gills are an unmistakable combination. This is particularly striking in view of the fact that the creature is purely air-breathing but nevertheless clearly posses gills, a sign that it has nothing to do with real animal life. It has four legs, a large tail, and a tongue, all of which appendages might be described as tentacles or tentacle-like. It has prominent ears that might be a caricature of a mouse's ears, but really more closely resemble the control surfaces on an airplane's tail.

When the father first sees the creature in his new apartment, he thinks it is vermin and tries to kill it, but he quickly becomes friends with it. The creature accompanies him everywhere he goes (except to his factory job). It seems that everyone, or at least every family, in the new city has such a creature for a companion, although each one is strikingly different in appearance. Most of the connections with strangers that the father makes come about at first through the creature's befriending the creature of the other person, in much the same way that two dogs who meet when being walked by their masters will make friends. Indeed, it seems as if the creature is purposefully looking out for the father's welfare to some degree, and purposefully integrating into the social network of the new city. In return it receives table scraps (specialized pet foods did not become common until after World War II).

Grocer

The grocer owns the business where the father first tries to buy food for himself. He demonstrates to the father that the food available in the new city is completely different from the food that he (and the reader) knows. He invites the father to his home to give him dinner and show how him how to prepare some of the unfamiliar food. Along the way, the grocer recalls the history of his family's escape from a city destroyed by the cyclopes. The grocer and his family are very hospitable to the father and in particular give him a jar full of what is probably wine, which the father keeps and which eventually becomes a bird's nest on his window sill, symbolizing the renewal of the cycle of life the father finds in the new city.

Grocer's Son

The grocer first singles out the father for special hospitality after his son (who helps him in his shop) befriends the father's animal.

Grocer's Wife

The grocer's wife was with him during their escape from their destroyed city and takes a leading part in the hospitality the grocer shows to the father.

Immigrant Man

The father asks a stranger on the street where he might find a room, communicating by drawing in his notebook. Like almost everyone depicted in the new city, this man is also an immigrant, but from a country different from the father's.

Immigrant Woman

At the end of the story, the father's child befriends a newly arrived immigrant woman, creating the largest of *The Arrival*'s cycles of renewal.

Landlady

The landlady of the building where the father takes a room has an especially bizarre familiar animal that momentarily frightens the father. It is this encounter that first lets the reader grasp the kind of relationship that exists between the human characters and their companions.

Mother

The father's sojourn to the new city is largely for the benefit of his wife and their child, in other words his family. The mother makes a much greater display of grief at their separation than the father does, since, as in the Western culture of a century ago, women's feelings in their culture can be less constrained than those of men. Since the father is probably leaving because of poverty in their home city, her situation will only become worse as she waits for her husband to send for her. When she and her child finally land in the new city, she is clearly apprehensive before they find the father. But, significantly, her expression of rejoicing is not shown when they do so, or until the coda of the book after they have been settled in for some time and the family is reestablished to her satisfaction. Just as the father is delighted by his social networking in the new city, she is delighted by homemaking.

Sign Hanger

The father's first job comes when he talks a sign hanger into letting him finish his day's work for a part of his salary, a very common way for the economically marginal to both find work and begin to make connections with the worker he subcontracts from and potentially with that person's employer.

Freedom

The first person in the new city whose life story the reader of *The Arrival* learns about is the ex-slave who helps the father buy an aerial bus ticket. As a young girl, she was forced to work in some kind of industrial facility. She was pointedly denied the freedom to learn by her masters. One could see this situation as an allegory of economic oppression and its stifling of human growth, if one considered slavery to be a thing of the past. One could easily relate the woman's story to the industrial slavery practiced by the Nazi régime, a reflection of the horrors of the past. But, in fact, there are today at least twenty-seven million slaves in the world, more than at any time in the past. While many are women and children forced to work in the sex industry, many others are victims of debt bondage. Debt slavery is especially common in South and Southeast Asia. It may be that after a famine, a farmer had to take a loan from a moneylender, and after a second bad harvest was unable to pay it back. After another bad year, the moneylender, through the use of compound interest, can lay claim to the farmer's entire crop and can tack more onto the farmer's debt for the small amount of food the moneylender gives back to him from the harvest to ward off starvation. As the debt grows past any possibility of ever being paid, the moneylender lays claim to all the labor of his client, effectively making him a slave. The moneylender can then sell his client to a business, where he will be forced to work in dangerous and degrading labor, or else go to jail for failure to pay debts. This is most likely the kind of labor being performed by the ex-slave in *The Arrival*. Moreover, the burden of debt is passed on from generation to generation, so that many people in slavery in India or Pakistan today are supposedly working to pay off an original debt of a few dollars incurred by an ancestor in the nineteenth century.

Tan undoubtedly condemns the morally repugnant reality of slavery in *The Arrival*, even if he leaves its relationship to the real world and the modern world ambiguous. In that sense he could not more fiercely champion freedom, but he also displays a curious attitude toward liberty. When the father's ship reaches the new city, he sees what is identifiably the New York skyline (pages 20–21), except that the Statue of Liberty has been replaced by a statue showing two friends from different cultures reaching out to shake hands, a symbol of community. Although community and liberty are both widely recognized as virtues, they are to a degree antithetical. To the degree that one cooperates with another, even for the sake of mutual aid, one gives up that same degree of freedom under the weight of responsibilities and commitments. Clearly there is a continuum, rather than a true opposition, between the freedom of the individual and his responsibility to others. Still, the switch of statues shows Tan supporting communal virtues over individual ones. This would not be exceptional, except for the expectations encouraged by *The Arrival*'s reputation as a surrealist work. Liberty held a special place in the thought of the surrealists.

Topics for Further Study

- Michael Chabon's 2000 Pulitzer Prize–winning *The Amazing Adventures of Kavalier and Clay* treats many of the same themes as *The Arrival*. It deals both realistically and metaphorically with the immigration to the United States of refugees from the Nazi conquest of Western Europe. The backdrop of the story is the early comic book industry. Surrealism has a prominent place in the book, and Salvador Dalí appears as a character. It deals with how identity is based on memory, but also how memory must be abandoned to find new identities. Read the book and write an essay comparing the treatment of some of these themes in the two novels.

- *Exquisite Corpse* is a game invented by the surrealists to demonstrate the creative power of the human subconscious. Organize a few rounds of it among your classmates, splitting them into groups of five or six. To play, the group leader writes out on a sheet of paper a column of the names of the parts of speech in an order that makes a sentence, like so: article _____ noun _____ verb _____ article _____ noun _____. More complicated patterns can also be used. The paper is handed around to each member of the group who writes down an actual word of the indicated kind on the line, then folds the paper so the next player cannot see what was written before and passes it on, until the sentence is complete. The leader then reads what was written, makes any necessary adjustments for agreements of number or case, and reads out the randomly created sentence. The title of the game is itself a striking phrase created by this kind of random generation that would be most unlikely to have been made up on purpose.

- Research modern forms of slavery using Internet resources and make an illustrated PowerPoint presentation to your class on the subject. Some places to start might the websites of the United Nations Office of the High Commissioner for Human Rights (http://www.ohchr.org/Documents/Publi sites devoted to international news and studies like the BBC (http://news.bbc.co.uk/2/hi/africa/75764 or the Asia Pacific Project at the University of California at Berkeley (http://journalism.berkeley.edu/projects/a

- *The Arrival* is not the only graphic work to deal with the theme of immigration for young adults. Many immigrant artists from Latin America and the Far East deal more or less directly with the subject. Two interesting examples are a series of comic strips by Henry Kiyama about the experience of Japanese immigrants to San Francisco between 1904 and 1924, which have been collected and translated and by Frederik L. Schot in the 1999 *The*

Four Immigrants Manga, and the comic strips about their immigrant experience that are assigned to immigrant students at Oakland International High School, of which a selection have been published in the 2012 volume *We Are Oakland International*. With works like these as models, use the graphic serial form to tell the immigrant story of your own family, bearing in mind that everyone living in North America is descended from immigrants, even if the immigration took place hundreds or thousands of years ago.

In the original "Manifesto of Surrealism" (1924), almost the only traditional virtue that André Breton (the leader of the Surrealist movement) does not condemn, but even praises, is liberty: "The mere word 'freedom' is the only one that still excites me." It is only liberty—the liberty that exists inside every individual—that sustains the surrealist and, indeed, the human spirit:

> Among all the many misfortunes to which we are heir, it is only fair to admit that we are allowed the greatest degree of freedom of thought. It is up to us not to misuse it.

Of course the surrealists were famous for their collaborative efforts, for example in joint shows and exhibitions put on by the surrealist movement as a whole. But it is clear that their emphasis lay in the opposite direction from Tan's. For the surrealists, the most important thing was artistic individuality. For Tan the most important thing is a supportive and sustaining community.

Language and Languages

The new city to which the father goes uses a language unknown to him. He can communicate with its inhabitants only through drawings and gestures, and when he gets a job hanging posters written in the language, he hangs them upside down because he cannot read the script. In fact, the script is prominently shown throughout the story on signs and in paperwork. It is, for the most part, unrelated to any real writing system. Although the letter forms in many cases resemble those of alphabetic scripts, the lack of repetition of characters would suggest they are logograms like Chinese characters where each character stands for a separate word. To a degree this is comparable to the creation of artificial writing systems such as those in J. R. R. Tolkien's *The Lord of the Rings*. However, Tan's characters do not seem to be a functional writing system, in the sense that it cannot be deciphered, transliterated, and translated into English. Rather, its texts exist merely to show the father's perplexity in not being able to understand the language of the place where he lives, a common feature of the immigrant experience. An exception seems to be first title page of the book, written in the unknown language. In this case the words *Arrival* and *Shaun Tan*, written in the foreign script, can be deciphered since each letter is a manipulation of the corresponding English letter (i.e., inverted, cut in half, with the individual pen strokes used to make the letter rearranged, et cetera) whose form is still recognizable.

Graphic Novel

The idea of telling story through a succession images, as if one were taking a photograph of some event every few seconds, seems a logical extension of making a single image to show a scene. But while the first paintings are almost 30,000 years old, virtually nothing that can be considered a graphic narrative, in the sense of a serial presentation of images telling a story, can be found before a thousand years ago. On the contrary, Western art traditionally created scenes in which several discrete moments in time were all shown together in a single image. But Mayan art experimented with sequences of images in the twelfth century. The Bayeux Tapestry (which told the story of the Norman Invasion of England in 1066 in the following decades) is also frequently cited as an early graphic narrative, but it was without influence or parallels in its time. Although political cartoons in newspapers sometimes assumed a serial form as early as the eighteenth century, the key stage in the development of the modern graphic format—the panel cartoon—seems to have been largely based on the development of motion pictures. Sets of postcards were published in the late nineteenth century that showed shots of models sometimes only a few seconds apart, allowing motion to be reconstructed. The next step was to take the photos more frequently and flip the cards more rapidly to give the illusion of motion. The first true projected films and the first comic strips appear at almost the same time (around 1890). Not coincidentally, the same person, Windsor McCay, created both the first recognizably modern comic strip (*Little Nemo*) and the first successful film cartoon (*Gertie the Dinosaur*). The comic strip, however, was quickly stereotyped as a trivial diversion or entertainment for children.

The surrealist Max Ernst created what can be described as an early graphic novel in his books of collages. Before photographic printing became commonplace, newspapers and magazines were illustrated with engravings that could be easily and cheaply printed. Ernst would take such images, cut out various elements from different samples, and then paste them together in novel relationships to each other to create new meanings. He published whole books of such images carrying narratives over dozens of pages, including *The Woman with 100 Heads* (*La femme 100 têtes*, 1929) and *A Week of Kindness* (*Une semaine de bonté*, 1934). Significantly, Ernst's images were shown entirely without words or description. Largely uninfluenced by Ernst (but influenced by Japanese *manga*, comics which seem to have evolved largely independently out of traditional woodcuts and which always dealt with serious artistic themes), American comic artists in the 1980s and 1990s employed to create super-hero comic books for children began to produce more intellectually challenging work meant for an adult audience. Their work was quickly termed *graphic novels* for the first time. The popularity of this form allowed for the publication of more experimental and innovative works like Tan's. Tan claims that *The Arrival* is directly indebted to surrealism, indicating his connection to Ernst. But a more important influence on Tan seems to be old photograph and postcard series. He simulates these, for example, in many full-page panel series that suggest photographic sequences showing action every few seconds. His return to these early sources, and his detachment from the comic book stream of graphic storytelling, is reflected also in his abandonment of language in *The Arrival* and his complete dependence on a visual narrative.

Influence

Ordinary literature is filled with examples of an author writing a new passage based on an earlier text, transforming the source into a new work of art. In Shakespeare, for instance, Macbeth's lament over the death of his wife is closely based on passages from the biblical books of Job and the Psalms, while Prospero's farewell speech at the end of *The Tempest* is a reflection of the work of the Roman poet Ovid. Another example is the seventh chapter of Oscar Wilde's *The Picture of Dorian Gray*, in which Wilde rewrites passages from various museum catalogs and guide books. In the visual arts this can be compared, for example, to the technique of Peter Paul Rubens, many of whose painted figures are based on classical statues. The surrealist

Max Ernst expanded on this technique, making the first graphic novels out of collages compiled from existing magazine and book illustrations. In his afterword to *The Arrival*, Tan describes using the same technique in his own work. Many of his illustrations are closely based on photographs or engravings that he has adapted to his specific needs and themes. Specific images that he used in this way include Tom Roberts's 1886 painting, *Going South* (on display at the National Gallery of Victoria, Melbourne; compare page 17 in *The Arrival*), and Gustave Doré's 1872 engraving *Over London by Rail*, to which Tan has added threatening shadow tentacles on pages 6 and 7. He also used many photographs, including one of a newsboy selling the paper that announced the sinking of the *Titanic* in 1912 (the first panel on page 34). More generically, he used postcards depicting New York from a century ago (on pages 20–22), as well as photographs documenting the processing of immigrants at Ellis Island (on pages 23–27), as well as photographs possibly documenting the devastation of Europe after World War II (page 95). He does not merely copy these images, but transforms them (as he says in an interview with Karen Haber in *Locus*): I don't think I've ever painted an image as a reproduction of what I'm seeing, even when I'm working in front of it. I'm always trying to create some kind of parallel equivalent, a serious caricature that emphasizes a particular idea or feeling about the subject.

Historical Context

Human history has always been a history of migration. As soon as modern humans evolved in Africa about 100,000 years ago, there was a wave of migration around the Indian Ocean as far as Australia, and about 50,000 years ago, a second wave that populated the rest of the world, to the southern tip of South America. Movement between human groups has meant that no population has ever become isolated, so that no races in any meaningful scientific sense have arisen. The brotherhood of man that Tan celebrates in *The Arrival* has been maintained by migration. But Tan is most directly concerned with the history of migration in the twentieth century (and to avoid confusion, *emigration* is to leave one's old home, while *immigration* is to come into one's new home). The Arrival tells the story of a man who leaves his home to go to a new country where there is better economic opportunity, and who sends for his family to come after him when he has reached a higher level of prosperity than he could have had at home. This is a story that played out millions of times (though often the whole family went together) in the nineteenth and early twentieth centuries, in response to the exponential growth of the world economy in the industrial revolution, creating wealth in some countries and disaster in others (the potato blight that caused the Irish famine of the 1840s, of instance, was introduced by international trade).

People moved from poverty to prosperity. The largest part of this movement, and the most emblematic, was from Europe to the United States, much of it coordinated through the Ellis Island Immigrant Inspection Station. The Statue of Liberty was erected on nearby Bedloe's Island as a symbol of the American freedom and opportunity that were sought after by economic migrants from Europe. The immigration procedure gone through by the father in *The Arrival* minutely recreates the Ellis Island experience and is based on photographic records kept there, which Tan traveled to New York to study. In Tan's world, however, the Statue of Liberty has been replaced by a monument to friendship and brotherhood, suggesting that for him the ideals of community are more important than individual ideals.

Before and after World War II, Europe saw a vast emigration of political refugees, fleeing either the Nazis or the Communist regimes established by Stalin in Eastern Europe. Tan deals with this subject also, in the family that fled the destruction of their city by the cyclopes.

Tan's native Australia also saw a large wave of immigration in the nineteenth and early twentieth centuries, from Britain and its empire and, to a lesser degree, from continental Europe. Tan pays tribute to this in the use he makes of Tom Roberts's painting *Going South* (page 17), which commemorated English immigration to Australia. However, Tan's own family migrated from Malaysia to Australia, as did many Asians in the twentieth century. There seem to be no direct references to this immigrant experience, which can most clearly be said to be Tan's own, in *The Arrival*. Rather, it is as if he subsumes the experience of his own family under the better-known category of immigration to America.

Critical Overview

Before the publication of *The Arrival* in 2006, Tan already had a worldwide reputation as a children's book illustrator, so the new work was widely and favorably reviewed and also became the focus of a large number of interviews with the author as part of the publicity associated with a major book release. The *New York Times* review ("Stranger in a Strange Land") was written by Gene Luen Yang, himself a distinguished Chinese American graphic novelist. Yang begins by emphasizing that *The Arrival* is indeed a graphic novel and must be treated as such (particularly in regard to shelving in bookstores, since narrative graphic works by established children's authors are too often treated as story books). He notes that Tan paradoxically achieves intimacy by presenting his story in the most generic terms not pegged to a specific time, place, or language: "His drawings depict architecture and clothing that are at once historic and futuristic." Since America's is the most generic (because the best-known) history of immigration, "by borrowing American imagery to communicate an otherwise universal story, Tan highlights just how central the immigrant experience is to the way America defines itself." Yang sees some difficulties in stylistic holdovers from Tan's work as a mere illustrator:

> The sheer beauty of Tan's artwork sometimes gets in the way of his

narrative. His panels, like the best photographs, capture the timelessness of particular moments, which can inadvertently endanger the illusion of time passing that a graphic novelist strives to create.

The Arrival has also received some attention in the scholarly literature. Though more directly concerned with Tan's *Tales from Outer Suburbia*, Rebecca-Anne C. Do Rozario, writing in *Marvels & Tales* in 2011, has drawn attention to the fantastical nature of *The Arrival*'s urban landscapes, and especially to the strange experiential quality of reading a detailed narrative without words. In the 2011 issue of the *Children's Literature Association Quarterly*, Julia L. Mickenberg and Philip Nel characterize the openness with which the father is received as a new immigrant as a countercultural political statement: "Following the post–9/11 suspicion of people from other countries, *The Arrival* goes against the grain of both US and Australian Immigration policies." So far, the most extended treatment of *The Arrival* is Michael D. Boatright's 2010 article in the *Journal of Adolescent & Adult Literacy*. Boatright considers *The Arrival* together with other recently published graphic novels that concern the immigrant experience that are readily available for use in school classrooms. He also considers that the prominence of immigration issues in American politics makes *The Arrival* a topical subject of study. Boatright deconstructs the story of *The Arrival*, attacking it for presenting a male, white, European immigrant who achieves success without breaking the laws of his new country, which Boatright views as a politically oppressive attack against more-recent immigrants to the United States.

What Do I Read Next?

- Tan's 2000 short book *The Lost Thing* establishes much of the style and many of the visual conventions for *The Arrival*. In 2010, Tan directed an adaptation of *The Lost Thing* as an animated cartoon and won the Oscar for Best Animated Short Film.

- Gene Luen Yang's 2006 *American Born Chinese* is a graphic novel for young adults about the experience of the Chinese American immigrant community.

- In her 2001 *Dragon Seed in the Antipodes: Chinese-Australia Autobiographies*, Yuan-fang Shen creates a history of the Chinese immigrant community in Australia from a close reading and commentary of more than twenty autobiographical documents going back to the nineteenth century.

- *The Secret Life of Salvador Dalí* (originally published in 1942 and reprinted in 1993) recounts the great surrealist artist's experiences as an immigrant to America fleeing Fascism in Europe and also gives an in-depth discussion of surrealist ideology and aesthetics.

- Wendy Lowenstein and Morag Jeanette Loh's 1977 book *The Immigrants* offers a series of case studies of immigration to Australia and was used by Tan as source material while creating *The Arrival*.

- *Sketches from a Nameless Land* is a fifty-page commentary on The Arrival by Tan, along with preliminary sketches. It had been published separately and bound together with *The Arrival* since 2010, but as of 2012 it has not been distributed outside of Australia.

Sources

Bales, Kevin, *New Slavery: A Reference Handbook*, 2nd ed., ABC-Clio, 2004, pp. 71–96.

Benton, Barbara, *Ellis Island: A Pictorial History*, Facts on File, 1985, pp. 48–131.

Boatright, Michael D., "Graphic Journeys: Graphic Novels' Representations of Immigrant Experience," in *Journal of Adolescent & Adult Literacy*, Vol. 53, No. 6, March 2010, pp. 468–76.

Breton, André, "Manifesto of Surrealism (1924)," in *Manifestoes of Surrealism*, translated by Richard Seaver and Helen R. Lane, University of Michigan Press, 1972, pp. 1–47.

———, *What Is Surrealism?*, translated by David Gascoyne, Faber & Faber, 1936, pp. 9–24.

Christiansen, Hans-Christian, "Comics and Films: A Narrative Perspective," in *Comics & Culture: Analytical and Theoretical Approaches to Comics*, edited by Anne Magnussen and Hans-Christian Christiansen, Museum Tusculanum Press, 2000, 107–21.

Dalí, Salvador, *50 Secrets of Magic Craftsmanship*, translated by Haakon M. Chevalier, Dover, 1992, pp. 33–39.

———, "The Phenomenon of Ecstasy," in *The Collected Writings of Salvador Dalí*, edited and translated by Haim Finkelstein, Cambridge

University Press, 1998, p. 201.

Docker, John, and Gerhard Fischer, eds., Race, *Colour and Identity in Australia and New Zealand*, University of New South Wales Press, 2000, pp. 113–73.

Dodson, Howard, "Slavery in the Twenty-First Century," *UN Chronicle* Online Edition, May 5, 2008, http://www.smfcdn.com/assets/pubs/un_chronicle.pc (accessed March 30, 2012).

Do Rozario, Rebecca-Anne C., "Australia's Fairy Tales Illustrated in Print: Instances of Indigeneity, Colonization and Suburbanization," in Marvels & Tales: *Journal of Fairy-Tale Studies*, Vol. 25, No. 1, 2011, pp. 13–32.

Ernst, Max, *The Hundred Headless Woman = La femme 100 têtes*, George Braziller, 1981.

———, Une semaine de bonté: A Surrealistic Novel in Collage, Dover, 1971.

Groensteen, Thierry, "Why Are Comics Still in Search of Cultural Legitimization?" in *Comics & Culture: Analytical and Theoretical Approaches to Comics*, edited by Anne Magnussen and Hans-Christian Christiansen, Museum Tusculanum Press, 2000, pp. 29–41.

Haber, Karen, "Shaun Tan: Out of Context," in *Locus: The Newspaper of the Science Fiction Field*, December   2001, http://www.locusmag.com/2001/Issue12/Tan.html (accessed March 25, 2012).

Margolis, Rick, "Stranger in a Strange Land," in *School Library Journal*, September 2007, p. 34.

Mickenberg, Julia L., and Philip Nel, "Radical Children's Literature Now!," in *Children's Literature Association Quarterly*, Vol. 36, No. 4, Winter 2011, pp. 445–73.

Nielsen, Jesper, and Søren Wichmann, "America's First Comics? Techniques, Contents, and Functions of Sequential Text-Image Pairings in the Classic Maya Period," in *Comics & Culture: Analytical and Theoretical Approaches to Comics*, Anne Magnussen and Hans-Christian Christiansen, eds., Museum Tusculanum Press, 2000, pp. 59–77.

Tan, Shaun, *The Arrival*, Arthur A. Levine, 2006.

———, "Teacher's Book Notes: *The Arrival*," Scholastic   website, http://www.scool.scholastic.com.au/schoolzone/tooll (accessed March 12, 2012).

"Tom Roberts, *Coming South* 1885–86," in *Exiles and Emigrants: Educational Resource*, http://www.ngv.vic.gov.au/exilesandemigrants/ed_jc (accessed March 23, 2012).

Yang, Gene Luen, "Stranger in a Strange Land," in *New York Times*, November 11, 2007, http://www.nytimes.com/2007/11/11/books/review/' t.html?_r=2 (accessed March 25, 2012).

Further Reading

Davies, Will, and Brosco Dal, *Tales from a Suitcase: The Afghan Experience*, Lothian, 2002.

> Cited as a source for *The Arrival* by Tan, this book, later made into a televisions series in Australia, tells the story of Afghan refugees from the Soviet invasion of their country who immigrated to Austrailia.

Descharnes, Robert, and Gilles Néret, *Salvador Dalí 1904–1989: The Paintings*, Taschen, 2002.

> This is the latest incarnation of Descharnes's catalog of Dalí's complete works and includes not only all of his paintings, but all of his major works in other media (including photos of his surrealist objects as well as the photographs staged at his direction). It is a unique documentation of the history of surrealist painting.

Tan, Shaun, *Tales from Outer Suburbia*, Arthur A. Levine, 2009.

> Tan's latest full-length book, this volume explores the irruption of the inexplicable into everyday life, using Tan's typical mixture of cartooning and nearly photo-realistic images.

Yarwood, A. T., *Attitudes to Non-European Immigration*, Cassell, 1968.

> For over a hundred years, immigration to Australia was limited by what is known as the White Australia Policy, which limited immigration to the country from outside of Europe, in support of a racist and imperialist Australian government. In 1973 this law was ended, leading to a massive influx of Asian economic migrants. This history of Australian race policy was written on the eve of the country's overthrow.

Suggested Search Terms

Shaun Tan

Shaun Tan AND The *Arrival*

Shaun Tan AND graphic novel

Shaun Tan AND surrealism

immigration

Ellis Island

refugees

automatic drawing